Where the English Housewife Shines

Where the English Housewife Shines

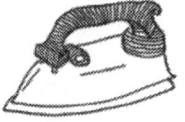

Alexandra Oliver

TIN PRESS, LONDON

HAMM:
Nature has forgotten us.

CLOV:
There's no more nature.

HAMM:
No more nature! You exaggerate.

CLOV:
In the vicinity.

HAMM:
But we breathe, we change! We lose our hair, our teeth! Our bloom! Our ideals!

CLOV:
Then she hasn't forgotten us.

-Samuel Beckett, *Endgame*

Published in 2007

Copyright © Alexandra Oliver Basekic

All rights reserved.

All poems and illustrations by Alexandra Oliver
Typeset by The Tin Press v3.1

Where the English Housewife Shines

Published by:
The Tin Press
12 Rudolf Place
Miles Street
London, SW8 1RP
www.tinpress.co.uk

ISBN 978-0-6151-4436-8

Contents

Phone Sex	9
The Tie	12
Ring-a-Ding-Ding	15
Ballad of the Frontal Lobe	18
Love, Like at the Bank	23
Stars	24
Pharmacy Poem	37
Not Ovid	39
The Bad Joke	40
For the Sensualist	41
Grass	42
Enjoy this Villanelle	44
How to Be a Team Player	45
Bible Story	48
Richard Burton	49
Hair Song	50
Blessing	53
Sunset Lands in Houston	54
I Beg You	55
Seven Thousand Francs	57
Pioneer Square	59
The Immigrant Worker's Wife's Villanelle	62
Villanelle for Isabelle Dinoire	63
Terence Stamp	64
Ned's Trainers	66
The Smell of Trouble	68
Love	69
Death and Las Vegas	71

Phone Sex

Hello, my name is Mary Lou,
Your phone sex partner for tonight.
I'm five-foot four, blue-eyed and white.
My legs are fat, my chest is flat,
And, though my teeth are fairly bright,
I have horrendous overbite,
A running nose and bunching hose;
My perfume smells like burning roast,
I have more facial hair than most,
And have the privilege to boast
Apocalyptic taste in clothes.

My hair is kind of sewage brown
And, when I choose to wear it down,
It never fails to astound
Prospective customers and mates
With how the greasy coating weights
It down on either side;
In fact, I take enormous pride
In being able, still, to speak
Of how, through washing once a week
By mixing half a cup of Tide,
A glass of milk, a box of yeast,

And half a tablespoon (at least)
Of taxidermy formaldehyde,
My scalp erupts in oozing boils
Which, as they start to then ferment,
Emit a heady pungent scent
As found within the richest soils.

My body's fairly bulletproof
And, had it not been for that goof,
The Swedish count in Tanzania
(Who gave me awful gonorrhea),
My health would be completely sound,
Though certain germs do get around,
And when, last year, the doctor found
That plethora of creeping warts
Upon my legs I was, or course,
A little bit dismayed.

My God, the difference acid made.

I do acknowledge how it bores
When I reiterate my stores
Of sprouting moles, enormous pores,
And fifteen open running sores,
Clubfoot, harelip, tennis wrist,
Gingivitis, facial cyst,
And if there's anything I've missed,
I'm sure your mind is well equipped.

So, while your fly is now unzipped,
Let me take the time to say,

It doesn't matter how you pay:
Your Visa number and the day
You think it might expire…

And now I've set your loins on fire,
Thank you for a lovely time.

There's someone on the other line.

The Tie

Back when I was only ten,
My mum and dad decided
I was a vermin in the den
Where all of us resided.
I lacked an upper-class finesse,
Was full of temperamental rage,
Was bad at sport and couldn't dress,
The ostrich in the gilded cage.
I lacked a fundamental tool;
They sent me off to boarding school
To make some friends my age.

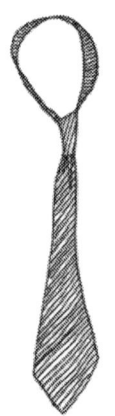

I wish to God they'd pierced my heels
And left me on a hill to die;
Imagine how a child feels
To wear a polyester tie.
It was slick and cheap maroon,
Like something down my shirt had bled.
At night I crushed it like a prune
And threw it underneath my bed,
My bloody, polyester noose;
My tongue grew angry, fast, and loose,
And this is where it led.

Encircled by the crimson grip,
My throat became a virgin spring
For every sharp, sarcastic quip
And prepubescent serpent's sting.
Was I punished? Need you ask?
I of many open defects,
Nipped at bud and put to task,
Ironing linen for the prefects.
Every weekend, dawn 'till late,
I stood at my board in state,
Queen of all the social rejects.

One day, having done the whites,
A strange epiphany was nigh:
I felt an urge to be at rights
With my disgusting crimson tie.
I laid it down from right to left;
So full of moral zeal was I,
My mind, I fear, was not so deft
To note the setting was too high.
My eyes, they focused into space,
My wrist was light, my spirit soared,
A smile shone upon my face,
I cast it down, and then I roared—
The scarlet tie, which once I feared,
Was in retreat and being smeared
Back and forth across the board.

What an errant act to sin in:
My synthetic red appendage
With an iron set for linen
Liquefied beyond all mendage!

My attempt to love my tie
Was suffocated at its birth,
And today I cannot lie
In saying that it had no worth
(Except to say it was the lid of
That perverse Pandora's Box
I was lucky to be rid of,
Like braces, lice, and chicken pox.)
And so the fateful story ends:
I ran away from boarding school
And have decided on a rule,
Even though I have no friends:

Love your parents, though their needs
Form a horror which reminds you
Who is led and who is leader;
Take it by the throat, dear reader.
Going forth to meet your needs
Shouldn't be that which unwinds you
Like the way your parents do;
Just remember, only you
Can truly melt the tie that binds you.

Ring-a-ding-ding

I love a man who wears a ring
And offers up a round of drinks,
Enchanted, like the rites of spring,
And enigmatic like the Sphinx
With a boyish, disorderly forelock
Who, caught in a fatal wedlock,
Offers up what every truant thinks:

I'm a home-wrecker, baby,
I'm Julie Andrews' nightmare.
When other kids read Nancy Drew,
I was reading Flaubert.

I knew it at an early age
Whilst with my mother at the zoo;
I saw the pandas in the cage
And saw the cage but counted two.
I realized, to ease my cares,
In climbing those pubescent stairs,
The only thing on which to swing
Was living for dividing pairs.
Part two: according to you,
I grew into a dame who loved the shame

Of loaded guns and cheap affairs.
I'm a home wrecker, baby.
A man-usurping longhair.
You're the barn behind the house
And I'm the one to go there.

Let's do it for the hell of it,
The Aqua Velva smell of it.
I know you'll never tell of it
To your domestic pillar;
It's so very Henry Miller
And I know I'm only filler.
Like you really could compare us;
It's like standing Milo's Venus
Next to eighties Phyllis Diller.

I'm a home-wrecker, baby.
I'm spiritually threadbare.
I'm a flaming tart and she's
An angel in an armchair.

So darling, go ahead,
It's leave-it-in-the-lurch-day!
Will she find out when you are dead
And what will the church say?
You should go ahead and flaunt it,
Right before it fossilizes,
Since you obviously want it
And I've had it with surprises.
What's a few regretful hours
To the field of purple flowers?

Who's concerned with earning trust?
It's the Free Love Magic Bus!
It's organic, fresh and groovy!
There's no need to be concerned,
It's so obvious I've learned
That her body is a temple
And that mine's a drive-in movie.

I'm a home-wrecker, baby.
I'm really glad to be here.
Get your hand from off my knee
And ask him for the check, dear.

And so, thank you for the drink.
This has really been a treat;
Life is luminous and pink
When you're traitorously sweet
Like the moon above the street
Upon which the lover ruminates,
The same one which illuminates
The dishes in her sink,
And it really makes me think…

It's so hard to swallow strife,
But I'd rather not compete.
You will need a sharper knife
If you want to cut my meat.
It's a lonely sort of life;

Now go home and fuck your wife.

The Ballad of the Frontal Lobe

How nice it is to have a brain,
That grey, electric, pulsing mass
That tells you when to catch your train,
Or what to bring to Monday's class.
It functions pretty well until
You hit your head or get too ill,
Or someone, out behind your flat,
Assaults you with a baseball bat,
Steals your wallet, breaks your rib,
And leaves you eating with a bib.
I know it seems in awful taste
To view such prospects as a joke,
But now, with no more time to waste,
Let me tell you how I faced
The fallout from my mother's stroke.
You see, my mum was once a pile
Of pain, a blister filled with bile,
Until that day, I don't know how,
She went from homicidal cow
To all the patience of a Job
Because she lost her frontal lobe.

Way back when, when Mum got hitched
To Dad, who worked 'till after one,
She drank a lot of gin and bitched,
And after, when she had a son,
She bitched at him, but later switched
To bitch at Dad when, just for fun,
He knocked her up again. The frolic
Of her bouncing bags of colic
Drove her swooning to her bed
To brood and wish that she was dead
Until in '70, alack!
Again was lying on her back
In VGH Maternity,
Pumped to death with epidurals,
Bravely giving birth to me
And screaming, "I can't deal with three!"
Beneath the cheerful forest murals.
At eighteen months, I learned to run;
My mother wished she had a gun
And spent the days in dark regrets,
Her nights in tortured, wide-eyed sweats,
Clutching her viyella robe
Because she had a frontal lobe.

Mum was good at entertaining:
Good with flowers, good with wines,
Good at stoic overfeigning
Interest, good at witty lines,
Good at things which seemed so draining
(Where the English Housewife shines.)
Resplendent in her Pucci gown,

Mum, her smile like a clamp,
Would say between cemented teeth,
"Thanks for coming, Pat and Keith."
And, once the portals had swung shut,
Concluding the Patrician act,
Would, voice now growling from her gut,
Revert to acting like a nut.
The plates were tossed, the dog was smacked,
While I, pyjamaed on the stairs,
Would watch her crash amongst the chairs,
Until she turned and launched her flares
In one of her most poisoned stares
As blinding as a nightclub strobe,
Emitting from her frontal lobe.

I grew up, and Mum got worse.
You might expect a mellowing;
Four hours a day as friend and nurse,
The other twenty bellowing
And hitting people with her purse
At home, but outside helloing
And being achingly polite
While hating everyone in sight.
My dates who came were labeled proles
And raked upon the burning coals
And, being made to feel like dinks,
Are probably now seeing shrinks.
Manic highs, depressive diving,
Indy-level backseat driving,
Rage at fallen cakes or stains,
Comments on my skin or girth,

Speeding, getting drunk on planes,
Years of martyrish campaigns
And sneak offensives on self-worth
Took their toll. In '99
She has a stroke. Perhaps, as sign,
The damage done was most intense

Inside the hub of common sense,
The cockpit of the cranial globe
Referred to as the frontal lobe.

My mother, once so highly strung,
Went mellow almost overnight,
Abandoning her evil tongue
(She only lost it once while tight),
And friends, the old as well as young,
Found Mum an absolute delight.
Despite the fact, I have to tell,
Her memory was blown to hell,
Her mind was clearer than a bell,
And golly, did she listen well.
My mother, though now just as vague
As a defendant in The Hague,
Took to reading: Angelou,
Politics and Russian Drama,
Austen, Shelley, Steinbeck too;
I even caught her on the loo
With something by the Dalai Lama.

So, if you ask me honestly,
How all of this affected me,
I'd have to say, of my dad's wife,
Who now gets so much more from life,
I'd rather have an anal probe
Than give her back her frontal lobe.

Love, Like at the Bank

I had a friend who, on and off, for fun,
Would, out of the deposit slips, take one
And write down underneath, in forceful black,

GIVE ME THE MONEY,

Fold, and put it back.

It wound up, hours later, in the hand
Of someone's docile tweedy-suited grand-
Mamma in orthopedic heels.

The teller's face—

And *that* is how it feels.

Stars

Girl's Day magazine,
The rag of those of seventeen
And ninety, and those in between
Who want to know the current scene,
Is proud to now present, in print,
Our latest horoscopic stint:
The fantasies the mind defines
For twelve assorted astral signs.

I

Capricorn, the sensible,
Will court the reprehensible:
The solid shoes grammarian
Will take a young Librarian
And execute exotic kicks
Between the hours of twelve and six
But modify her carnal plays
From twelve to five on holidays,
When both of you dement yourselves
Beside the big, hydraulic shelves
And roll around like animals
With glassy, Dewey Decimals.

II

Aquarius, Aquarius,
So smart and so nefarious,
Undertakes the Classics Prof
With unrelenting smoker's cough.
You soon suggest Affairius
And render subject warius,
But soon, he'll cry, "carissimae!"
For coitus bellisimae.
The need to heavy petritus
Will lead to magnus detritus:
They'll sack him from the Chairius,
And you'll find that hilarious.

III

Pisces, the eternal dreamer,
Finds herself aboard the steamer
Bound for mystical Corfu,
And what a lucky break for you:
The hippie with the bronzen back
And Kama Sutra in his pack
Will share his undisclosed disease
Beneath the groaning olive trees
While dusty air inflates your lungs
And you discover with your tongues
The back of one another's throats
Amidst the roaming packs of goats.

IV

Aries, curly-headed ram
Will boldly don a dental dam
And butt her way into the psyches
Of two teenage girls in Nikes,
Spandex tops and baggy pants,
She spotted at the mall by chance.
By executing carnal fusion,
She will heighten their confusion,
Drive them both to tears and laughter,
Then take them out for doughnuts after.
It would happen to them one day;
They'll brag like hell at school on Monday.

V

Taurus, full of lusty bull,
Capitulates to passion's pull
To overtake and cheapify
The fitness trainer at the Y.
Listen how he sweats and stammers,
Dumber than a bag of hammers;
The acrid smell of Gatorade
Could wilt an iron barricade
As both divisions have it on
While heaving on the Gravitron.
Things like this are few and fewer;
"Just do it" never once rang truer.

VI

Gemini, your nature thrives
On alibis and double lives;
A pair of dentists soon arrives
On vacation from their wives.
The tilting chair, the rubber mask,
The laughing gas and—need you ask?—
One goes in to fix your filling
While the other one is drilling.
The whisper in a rasping rush
To stick with floss and change your brush.
Swinging girls are always fans
Of work-provided dental plans.

VII

Cancer, mistress of the home,
Permits her lusty eyes to roam
And land upon the hammerhead
Who's come to fix the garden shed.
Having offered lemonade,
You misdirect him to the shade
And mercilessly drive his wedge
Into your under-gardened hedge.
He's just an undeveloped yob
And this is just his summer job!
The moral: lads should guard their fruits
For unsubversive paper routes.

VIII

Leo drops her leaf of fig
While at a heavy metal gig
Having cornered four Arousers
Decked in wigs and plastic trousers.
"Come on, baby! On the bus!
There's one of you and four of us!"
But female sex appeal condones
The moss that gathers rolling stones.
The hell you wreak, as you are able,
Will make them split and leave the label
And reconsider M.T.V.
As "Maybe Try Vasectomy."

IX

Virgo, whiter than a sheet,
Blackens in the summer heat
And fires up her feral guns
Amidst a raving pack of nuns.
Fellini's eyes would just have bulged
To see the horror you indulged
In savoring the earthy smells
Behind the bolted doors of cells.
De Sade would thrash inside his cage
And grind his teeth in jealous rage
To redefine the joke moreover,
"What's black and white and red all over?"

X

Libra dances to the drum
Of perfect equilibrium,
And goes to conquer, *sans délai*,
The entire Cirque du Soleil.
Pulleys, wires, hooks and ropes
Intertwined with furtive gropes,
As you perform the dance of sleaze
Upon a madly swung trapeze,
Attended to your burning wrongs
By fifty men in sequined thongs.
A treat for those who won't consent
To sleeping out inside a tent.

XI

Scorpio, of rougher trade,
A porno star who hasn't made
A single film in twenty years
For reasons unbeknownst appears
In doorway of your college dorm
In brown UPS uniform.
After losing all but socks
And signing for each other's box,
You draw attention to his zip
And leave him with a decent tip.
Who cares what is or isn't right;
It had to be there overnight.

XII

Sagittarius, oh Reader,
Goes for some or other leader
From some unreferred-to nation
With a yen for domination.
Having managed to elate
By giving head to head of state,
And feeling in complete control,
(Engendered by the change of role),
She shoves him with an idle boot;
He trips upon his crumpled suit
And lands upon, in arabesque,
The scarlet button on the desk.

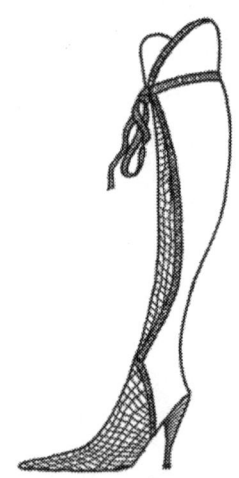

The Pharmacy Poem

There is nothing like a Really Awful Client
In a pharmacy that caters to the rich,
From the chauvinistic wiener
To the masochistic senior
To the rude and golden West Vancouver bitch.

There's nothing like a Really Awful Client,
Like the dowdy hippie matron in a sack
Who will put you through the burn
Of a thirty-buck return
And then tell you that she wants to take it back.

There is nothing like a Really Awful Client,
Like the person who, in halitosis vapor,
Starts demanding separate bills
For her douche and for her pills,
And then complains about the evil waste of paper.

There is nothing like a Really Awful Client,
Like the parent with the tot you want to slay;
There is nothing like the yelling
Of a child who is smelling,
Having barfed upon the windowfront display.

There is nothing like a Really Awful Client,
Like the moron whose opinion is unswerving:
Though he has a smaller brain,
He is higher on The Chain,
Because he's buying acne soap and you are serving.

There is nothing like a Really Awful Client,
But I guess it's just a test of human will;
Helping other people heal
Means the medicine is real,
But, although it does you good, it's still a Pill.

Not Ovid

Echo was a lovely maiden.
Narcissus was a foolish prat.
Echo's heart was passion-laden
But, when she begged, Narcissus spat.
She cried, as from a distant tower,
He ignored and she persisted.
He became a shoreside flower,
Consequence, as he resisted.
A cow came down to do some grazing
And bit his head off in the night.
Poetic justice is amazing;
Serve the stupid bugger right.

THE BAD JOKE

Billy had no limbs or body,
Just a Head upon the sill,
(Fate's allowance being shoddy)
Begging legs and arms until
God gave hearing to the knocker
At the door of Castle Heaven
Wanting only to play soccer
With other children of eleven.
God, enchanted with his praying,
Sent to Billy legs and arms,
(Generosity allaying,
But not swaying fatal harms.)
Billy leapt to find his luck,
Fast across the street he sped;
Got run over by a truck–
Better quit while you're a Head.

For the Sensualist

I met a man who made me think of cloves
And pepper on the eastern coastal air
And windy wheat that, cut, became the loaves,
And ginger in the wind that blew his hair.
Another made me think of bolts of silk;
Another of the oranges of Spain,
The shimmer of a stream of Jersey milk
And mushrooms that would mingle with the rain.
I never thought of socks or moldy bread,
Of sandwiches that lie around neglected,
That jobless wonder loafing in your bed
Who leaves you feeling cheap and disrespected.
So think about the world of useless oaves
And tell me if you smell the scent of cloves.

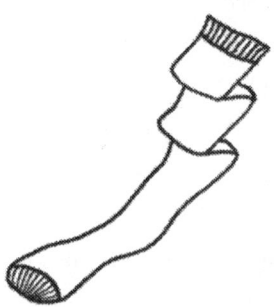

Grass

Hooray for splendor in the grass,
Where daisies, glads and lilies grow,
And branches swing and seasons pass
And water winds like twisted glass
From mountain springs of melted snow.

I was sitting by a stream,
Reading Coleridge, eating grapes,
When past me walked a poet's dream
Whose languid arms and cheeks of cream
Were whiter than my mother's drapes.

Both of us became enchanted
(Seven glasses, nothing less,
Of something stiff and well-decanted);
On my back I soon was planted
With his hands inside my dress.

Four months later, I grew fainter
Then I learned—and it surprised me—
How this git, who'd found a quainter
Blonde and buxom landscape painter,
Had wrecked my life and fertilized me.
Ladies, as the days grow fine,

Branches swing and seasons pass,
Heed a little warning line:
Tell your kids, as I tell mine,
Beware, beware, of booze and grass.

Enjoy This Villanelle

How a single word can so annoy!
It drives me so completely up the wall,
The use of the polite command *enjoy!*

Worst when sincere or just a trifle coy
In northern clip or sleepy southern drawl
How a single word can so annoy!

A toady in an office with a ploy
Hands his boss a coffee in the hall
Bats his lashes and lisps out *enjoy!*

A yuppie mum with boredom forks a toy
Over to her kid, while in the mall;
How a single word can so annoy!

A hooker spots a sailor man (ahoy!)
And after ditching purse and parasol
Gives him seven minutes to *enjoy!*

And years ago, that horse rolled up to Troy
Arrows tilting at the city wall
What, you think, could even more annoy?
The Greek translation of the verb *enjoy!*

How to Be a Team Player

Today upon your graduation
From Lord Nimrod Secondary,
Let me share some information
You may all find necessary.

When you land the job you wanted,
Many of you may be daunted
By the fact your work success
Is dependent still, you see,
In the modern company
Through its quintessential layers,
By the need to be Team Players.

In spite of how the gig seduced you,
This may take some getting used to.
You may have to one day get along
With people who you may, in fact, find weird,
Like Laura, whose demented lunchroom chats
Revolve around *Survivor*, bridge and cats,
Or Ted who, on that day you're down with cramps,
Will corner you to share his book of stamps.

This is not the problem when you think
That working all alone would really stink.
But, somehow when the concept of The Team

Falls into the hands of some big cheese
You may as well be fighting at full steam
An outbreak of incurable disease.

And so, along with your pathetic wage,
It may be thus decided at this stage
That you and your co-workers have to bond
Including those of whom you're not so fond.

You may find yourself at sea at nine,
Marooned in some infernal conga line
Around The Queen of Diamonds' heaving decks
With fifty-seven Microsoft Execs,
Around a campfire, blind on Sleeman's Ale
And desecrating "Whiter Shade of Pale",
Knowing that you have to share a tent
With Frank, the guy in charge of all the mail,
His bongos and his heady goat-like scent.
You may have to spend your Friday nights
In combat with a string of Christmas lights
Or drawing up a window-front display
Depicting the destruction of Pompeii,
Using only Styrofoam and dolls,
And just because you didn't have the balls
To tell your boss you'd rather spend your time
Alone than recreating the sublime
In one of Port Coquitlam's biggest malls.

You may be asked to smile yourself to bits,
Stuff yourself at lobster buffet feedings,
Play pitch and putt with homicidal gits
In the midst of your divorce proceedings.
Sit though seminars entitled,

"How to Love Your Peers",
"The Happy Worker is the One Who Cares",
"Share Your Feelings!",
"Teamship For Careers",

Knowing that, when faced with questionnaires
("Are you an Eminem or Britney Spears?")
Or things involving "trust and letting go".
The naked calisthenics in the snow,
Or gauntlets wielding grim fraternal hugs,
You'd rather be beset upon by thugs
Or facing twenty years for dealing drugs
Than give away your spiritual goods
At some suspicious men's camp in the woods.

When's it over? When's it going to end?
When you discover you can't find a friend
In everyone you work with. That the thing
You do must be done with the conviction
That you can do the best you can
With everything you are; no-one can rank you
Based on this part of the corporate plan,
And yes, your boss may one day have to yank you—

But hold your waving pennant high
That says *I love the other guy*
Who gives it just as much as I
As cook or lawyer, nurse or spy,
But I can choose my own team,
Thank you.

BIBLE STORY

Abraham was sacrificing Isaac on the hill
When God came down and told him it was only just a drill.

Richard Burton

How do we remember Richard Burton,
Incendiary martyr of The Biz?
Pissed as newts behind the velvet curtain,
Rolling on the ground and roaring "LIZ!"

Hair Song

Hey sister, I can see I've reached your answering machine,
So let me take a minute now to tell you where I've been:
I went down to see the man who did my heart wrong
And, since he does yours too, I know we'll get along.
I found out from reception that he has a routine
From the socialite of sixty to the girl of seventeen.
So, though if this were movies, we'd be at each other's throats,
I'd rather give some beauty tips and then compare some notes.

He's a love stylist,
Love stylist,
Magic at the basin,
From the roots to the ends,
From the virgin to the raisin.
Love stylist,
Love stylist,
Body shampoo,
He's a roller set for paradise
And what about you?

And so on,
And so on,
And so on,
And so on.
I was happy when I met him and I thought we'd be friends;

I was sick of those relationships with flyaway ends,
And I'd had it with the static and the fabulous fakes
And the years of being caught with those embarrassing flakes.
He had bounce, he had swing and a fabulous sheen,
But the combination doesn't mean it's absolutely clean
And it's hard to see when somebody is coloring the facts,
'Cause I wanted something permanent and he said, "Relax!"

Love stylist,
Love stylist,
Pleasure denied,
'Cause he was long on the top
But he had something on the side.
Love stylist,
Love stylist, tip of the tongue
Of those who said, "It's not you
But, boy it makes you look young!"

And so on,
And so on,
And so on,
And so on.

Well, it's the cut that you see, but it's the product that sells;
("Gee your hair smells terrific! Are you seeing someone else?")
And it's enough to drive a woman white who's dealing with a liar
Who's foiling someone else when you are underneath the dryer,
And it's never the same as how it looks in the mag,
'Cause on her it's a bob and on you it's just a shag.
So I'm making sure that other girls, that they don't get shat upon,
'Cause I told two friends,

And they told two friends,
And they told two friends,
And they told two friends,
And so on,
And so on,
Love stylist,
Love stylist,
Razored by a pig,
And I would rather be alone
And I would rather wear a wig.

Love stylist,
Love stylist,
Take it from me,
'Cause I didn't look good
But neither does he.

And so on,
And so on,
And so on,
And so on.

'Cause I didn't look good
But neither does he.

Blessing

May the world of women open up before you,
The Rubaiyat's eternal golden gate;
May the brunettes and the blondes
Sever old romantic bonds
And be eagerly obliging for a date.

When you go to get your coffee or your cleaning,
May the girl behind the counter drop her eyes;
May you get what you deserved
When your tuna melt is served
With an order of ingratiating sighs.

May the willowy and pillowy adore you,
May they run to you in bison-like stampedes.
May they tear you limb from limb
And cry, "It's him! It's him! It's him!",
Having recognized a flower in the weeds.

May they never underestimate your meaning.
May the one who wins be gratefully inclined.
Never settle to be chaste;
It would only be a waste.
May you realize that I—but never mind.

Sunset Lands in Houston

George Bush International. The only
Airport that could make me feel lonely,
Opens up its arms to me. I'm back
(From my yearly Christmastime attack
On elderly and young related hordes
Who strike the most excruciating chords)
To giant, slab-like border guards with guns
And halls the ghost of OJ Simpson runs
That seem to hurtle down, in glass and grate,
The length of the entire Lone Star State.

A Mexican from Tijuana slaps
Polish on my shoes. My neighbor taps
His toe to Willie Nelson. In the bar,
The jet-lagged jockeys find themselves on par
With bleary bar-girls pouring on the rocks
And swimming with the never-changing clocks.
Outside, a little man with orange flags
Is matching the reflection of my tags;
He walks towards the skyline of his town
And waves the sun magnificently down.

I Beg You

Never make your heart an open book.
Never throw yourself at any man
Don't track him in the supermart with smiles
Or block him and his shopping in the aisles
To point out something printed on a can.
Never find his address in the book
And drive out there to, well, just take a look
As you'll get caught, and then he'll tell his mates
You're probably the spawn of Norman Bates.

Never make your heart an open book
Never tell the quarry all your fears.
Never say you're terrified of slugs
Or going bald and springing for those plugs
Unless you want it all to end in tears.
Your wretched, dark aversions to the elevator doors
Closing as you plunge on past those twenty-seven floors
Can stuff themselves, my friend, for I can tell you, in the end,
A man is full of panic and he has no time for yours.

Never make your heart an open book.
Never talk about the ones before.
Never blather on about your ex
His liver and the soul-destroying sex

You had upon his parents' bathroom floor.
Spare the details of your last divorce;
Though he may nod and sagely mutter, "Brute!"
It's tossing at him strange and bitter fruit
The bastard's never going to get a hoot
Out of who got the house, the kids, the horse.

Never make your heart an open book
Never tell your men folk how you feel
Never phone them up when you are high
And tell them that, without them, you would die
'Cause most would rather crush beneath a wheel
Or climb towards a mess of power lines
Than face another heap of Valentines,
A droning ballad, picnic in the park,
Or weepy tantric yoga in the dark.

I know it's hard to palate this, but I suggest you try.
We champion the truth, perhaps. But really, when it comes to chaps,
They seem to like it better when you lie.

Seven Thousand Francs

Thank you, God, for giving me this day of useless toil,
For getting up at 6 a.m. to burn the midnight oil,
For coffee with the flavor of a dank, bubonic trench
I drink to keep my spirits up in mediocre French.
I'm up to see the day come in with unrestrainèd thanks,
And most of it has got to do with seven thousand francs.

I love the smell of ninety people sweating on a train
(It's that, or park your ailing car in never-ending rain);
The women's skins are yellowing from bleak, fluorescent light
And overwork and seven packs of Marlboro a night.
They file off to pharmacies and companies and banks,
Rewarded every thirty days with seven thousand francs.

The windows are cemented shut, the doors have greasy knobs,
I photocopy half the day and phosphorescent blobs
Go floating through my vision, and I wonder by degrees,
With that, and how a never-vacuumed carpet makes you wheeze,
If I can take a holiday away from urban ranks;
Perhaps I can afford it on my seven thousand francs.

Thank you, God, for giving me this day of useless toil;
I hope that, when I'm buried under seven feet of soil,
My children and their children keep the horse before the cart

And don't go in for financing, and then forgetting, Art.
Men and women aren't as indestructible as tanks—
And life like this can fuck itself for seven thousand francs.

Pioneer Square

The night before I moved to Seattle,
My eldest brother gave me the following advice:

Whatever you're going to do down there
For God's sake stay out of Pioneer Square.
I admit I haven't had time to go
But I've heard things from people who know.

It's not the sort of nighttime place
You want to be caught at 3 am
Drunk as a lord and with egg on your face
Without the recourse of your numchucks or mace.

There are roaming gangs of Latin thugs
And teenaged prostitutes on drugs
Wigged-out bag guys in the alleys
Hungry lions chewing up old tires
On the fringe of seething garbage fires
And the noise from all those skinhead rallies.

Gold-digging wenches are writhing in trenches
And boy scouts are handing out favors on benches.

Renegade bands of gypsy imps
Are ripping off wallets from drunken sailors
And giving the spoils to Austrian pimps
With hair as big as Elizabeth Taylor's.
Hard core leather bars for sluts
Where buff young men with tiny brains
Swing back on forth on iron chains
Protruding out of their you-know-what's.
Unification Church recruiters,
Hurricane Katrina looters,
Cannibal Germans and customs officials
With underpants bearing their mother's initials,
Oversexed Italian game show masters
Butt heads with frat boys dumb as two-foot planks
US Navy divers waving iron tanks
Against the onslaught of Watusi spears
And lovestruck jocks lobotomized by tears.

Be on your guard for mudslides, toxic waste,
Helicopter rotors dropped in haste,
And British Royals with enormous ears.

North Korean operatives in jeeps
Hold vigils using Swiss night vision glasses,
Poised to scan the actions of the masses.

Beware, because misfortune never sleeps!

The jellyfish, the rattlesnakes and eels
Await between the muggings and the deals
Gone wrong, the needles and the smoking bong,

The rolled up dollar bill inside the schnozz
The Minotaur, Medusa and the throng
Of screaming flying monkeys over Oz.
So keep your asses out of Pioneer Square
But should you ever leave your cab or bike
And make the aforementioned hellward hike
Phone me up and tell me what it's like
And next time I can take the family there.

The Immigrant Worker's Wife's Villanelle

The rain has come for seven long weeks now
She, his wife, would rather have stayed There.
A crow is hunched above the heavy bough.

She leaves the house, tugs lower on her brow
The scarf that hides the boxwood-glossy hair
She hasn't washed for seven long weeks now.

At forty-five, she still does not know how
To speak this grating tongue, nor does she care.
I watch her from our room above the bough.

Her husband, asked, would quietly allow
Mah-jongg, a tea with friends, were she to dare;
She hasn't done for seven long weeks now.

Back home they had two horses and a cow,
Four trees that groaned with almond, plum and pear
Her fingers long for each lost laden bough.

Her slim legs skim the bridge's rail somehow
The ledge at dusk is quieter than prayer.
She has been gone for seven long weeks now.
The startled birds have fled the heavy bough.

VILLANELLE FOR ISABELLE DINOIRE

Hold up that chin, as all those others do.
Brace yourself against the winter chill;
Step out, step out, they are expecting you.

The stories in the papers delve into
Sensation: how you were your own dog's kill;
Hold up that chin, as all those others do.

The suicide attempt, they know that too
The public loves the heady pity-thrill—
Step out, step out, they are expecting you.

Human eyes will wince but hunt on cue
The mauled, the burned, the limbless and the ill.
Hold up that chin as all those others do.

It's not your face, it is your face. The true,
The beauty is compacted in your will.
Step out, step out, they are expecting you.

Be radiant in having made it through
The fire of flash. Your peace will make them still.
Hold up that chin as all those others do;
Step out, step out, they are expecting you.

TERENCE STAMP

The millennium's a bore
And the sixties offered more
In my halcyon and juvenile opinion,
And the plethora of factors
With regard to certain actors
Leads my mind towards a designated minion.
All my friends think I'm pathetic
In my choosing the aesthetic
Swinging over into provinces of camp,
For I've fallen for the stud
In the role of Billy Budd,
You're the virus in my blood,
Terence Stamp.

Well, you dyed your hair for *Blue*,
And it didn't matter two
Decades slipped away, like some ill-fingered noodle;
How my passion thundered strange
As you rode across the range
And I frothed like someone's rabies-tainted poodle!

Teorema made me nervous,
But you did a godly service

To a role that would have given Brando cramp
With bisexual appeal.
Can't we sit and make a deal?
I've been broken on the wheel,
Terence Stamp.

Well, it isn't so surprising
That my Scorpio is rising
(*The Collector* set my nether organs frying.)
Why not pick a perfect villain
If the broken heart is willin'
And you've had it up to here with further trying?
It's so comforting to know,
You're engaging with a pro,
Me and every other evil-loving tramp.
Call me up, abuse, infect me,
I need someone to protect me;
Won't you come and please collect me,
Terence Stamp.

Ned's Trainers

How many times do I have to tell you
To get rid of those trainers?

I'll buy you new shoes,
Buy you many pairs.
What are you doing on Saturday?
We'll go shopping.

Do I keep things my ex-girlfriends gave me?
I'm tired of hearing about Ned,
His hair and his nice bike
And his horrible installation art.
Those giant white boxes that light up
The Canada Council gives him money to build.
Did the Canada Council give him money
So he could buy you those trainers?

Those trainers are ugly,
For one thing, they're white
They're all white
And they're dirty.
What are you, a nurse?
They look cheap.

They age you.

And they make you look

Like you're going to start running

And I'm going to have to beg you to come back.

THE SMELL OF TROUBLE

The envelopes of powder keep on coming,
Snowing rashes in assistants' hands.
US rations rain Islamic lands;
CNN hails, falling sky! While bumming
Out the ordinary Joes and Janes
Who swear off letters and domestic planes.

The newsprint whispers horror, gently stains
The digits of the housewives. Little wonder
Markets fold and bearishly go under,
Crunching under slow commuter trains,
Whining, like an orphan, on their wheels
In the hour of work and morning meals.

This is how a normal person feels,
Tilts their nose to scents of eastern trouble.
A land of rock is bombed to dust and rubble
In the wake of army-issue heels.
We lose the scent at night. Returning cars
Trail out beneath dissolving seams of stars.

Love

Love is like a stale Twinkie;
Sickly yellow, soft and stinky.
Sweet and squishy to the eyes,
Full of putrid germy lies,
Once the golden shell is broken,
(Sinful pleasure simply token.)
Love is very much the same:
A nice light snack, a wicked game.
Who knew that my heart would break
When what I deemed a piece of cake
Became a mash of crumbs and slime
And, bit by bite, and over time,
Turned each sweet tooth in me rotten,
Joy and trusting now forgotten.
I might have guessed, I should have known
By that horrendous overtone
Embodied yellow, red and blue:
The Twinkie Man with his lasso,
Grinning, spinning and reminding
Of the nature of our binding.
Having found beneath the sponge,
Gobs of dark neurotic grunge,
Each confronts but wants to hide,

Plastic wrap is thrown aside,
And now we know, despite the show,
The promise of our shelf life lied.
And all I wonder now, of late,
Is how the wretched Twinkie fate
Came upon me, tried to con me
With your bullshit on my plate.

Twinkies rot, and love is mean;
What a Ding Dong I have been.

Death and Las Vegas

We've often thought about our parents dying
(Worst case scenario: the B & E,
Those chalky loops to show where they were lying
When some mute thug made off with their TV.)

I want my folks to leave this life in bliss:
The heart attack while watching dames in plumes
Or jungle show, amidst the dry ice hiss,
Or in the heart-shaped hot tubs in their rooms.

A hemorrhage from spending at the mall
Or one too many prime rib at a meal
When God's all-seeing pea-sized silver ball
Seeks out their fatal digits on the wheel.

Acknowledgements

Earlier versions of several of these poems were first published in the following literary journals and publications: Nexus, Orbis Rhyme International, The Atlanta Review, The Vancouver Sun, and In Hell's Belly and Future Cycle poetry. "The Smell of Trouble" appeared in About.Com's Poems After the Attack anthology. "How To Be A Team Player" was originally commissioned for CBC Radio in 2003. My thanks go out to the editors and anyone else involved.

No-apologies neo-classicist **Alexandra Oliver** was born in Vancouver, Canada in 1970. She has performed her work at events ranging from the National Poetry Slam to Lollapalooza and has been featured on CBC Radio as well as in the 1998 documentary *Slam Nation*. She has taught poetry in high schools, colleges and prisons. Her poems have appeared in numerous journals. She lives in Seattle.

photo by Diyah Pera

www.ingramcontent.com/pod-product-compliance
Lightning Source LLC
LaVergne TN
LVHW041714060526
838201LV00043B/724

www.ingramcontent.com/pod-product-compliance
Lightning Source LLC
LaVergne TN
LVHW041714060526
838201LV00043B/728